Key Principles
and Other Tools

for Evangel Field Coaches
and Evangel Assessor Coaches

Key Principles and Other Tools

*for Evangel Field Coaches
and Evangel Assessor Coaches*

· ·

Rev. Bob Engel

TUMI Press
3701 East Thirteenth Street North | Suite 100
Wichita, Kansas 67208

Table of Contents

Key Principles for Coaching

1. Make sure you have a clear understanding of expectations in the coaching relationship.

2. This is not a job put a co-laboring in the Gospel. Take time to know the church planter, his/her family, children, and team members. Family and personal character are critical for the task-oriented planter. Make sure there is good healthy family dynamics and a growing in the grace and knowledge of the Lord Jesus as a redeemed child of God.

3. Expect excellence from the planter. This includes prayer, any preparation work that has been assigned, and goals established prior to the Coaches meeting. Keep the church planter accountable to goals and assignments he/she has agreed to accomplish.

4. Though relationship is important, this is a meeting with the defined objective to guide the planter in their commissioned task to plant a church. Keep this allotted time as a professional time. Find a space in which both you and the planter can speak, listen, and focus.

5. Move the planter forward as you provide guidance. Not only review past action steps put be aggressive, in the Spirit, to set new actions steps. This is where you ask lots of questions and "pull out" of the planter what the Spirit is placing on his/her heart.

6. There is never not enough opportunity to encourage the planter. Celebrate a victory forward no matter how small. It is a guarantee that the spiritual enemy will do his part to bring discouragement. Always come prepared to share scripture words of endurance, promise, encouragement, identity in Christ.

7. Schedule your next meeting. Make sure you and the planter place a high priority on these meetings. If you have to reschedule, make sure you do it immediately.

Simple Checklist for the Field Coach
(Based on the 1-Year Evangel Charter)

1. In-person visit to Team Leader in first month.

2. Schedule time to pray regularly for Team and Team Leader by name.

3. Schedule monthly Team Leader meeting either by phone call or by visit.

4. Monthly report to sending authority (if applicable).

5. Schedule four PWRs with the last one a review and planning time for the next year. Submit Evangel Quarterly Field Report to Dean (if applicable).

6 Help Team Leader identify and recruit a potential team leader for a new church plant.

7. Ensure that church plant is plugged into an Association (e.g. Urban Church Association) or Network.

8. Plan for 1-year Antioch celebration.

Sample Questions for the Monthly Meeting

1. **Questions on the Team's Spiritual Growth and Community Life (Are they living as a called community?)**

   a. Are you and your team walking with the Lord, seeking God intently, and growing spiritually together?

   b. Are you and your team relating to each other in love, forgiveness, and unity? Do any conflicts exist which need to be resolved?

   c. Are you and your team remaining called and committed to its vision, united together around it? Is the team working well together toward its purpose?

   d. Are you and your team functioning as a gifted and serving body together, especially in your relationships with one another?

2. Questions on Their Vision Together (Are they clear in their vision, values, and goals?)

   a. Do you and your team understand its vision and can the members articulate it to each other, and those outside the team?

   b. Are you and your team able to articulate the values on which the Vision Statement was built and are you still committed to them?

   c. Because of your team's experience in ministry, does any part of the Vision Statement or Values need to be reconsidered or rewritten?

3. Questions on the Team's Ministry Process and Results (Are they functioning wisely and effectively in ministry?)

   a. What gains have you made as a ministry team in your church planting community during this past month?

   b. What are the greatest struggles you have had in implementing your vision?

   c. What do your present schedules (i.e., personal and team schedules) look like and how does each ministry activity contribute to your ministry vision? What adjustments need to be made?

d. What is the quality of your ministry relationships currently? What individuals and families ought to be given further and deeper investment? How will you accomplish this?

4. **Questions for the Team's Ministry Planning and Strategy for the Next Ministry Period (Are they clear on the next steps the Spirit has for them to take?)**

a. How do you and the team intend on changing/affirming its original strategic plan for ministry during the upcoming month? In other words, what goals do you need to pursue in order to ensure maximum progress toward your vision?

b. Do you and the team have assignments and dates to all your critical tasks in the plan, or at least set a date to establish these specific steps?

Sample Pre-Evangel Assessor Coach Information Letter

Greetings Evangel Assessor Coach,

Here is some information as you prepare to serve the church plant team you will be coaching/assessing at Evangel.

1. Attached is a schedule of the Evangel School of Urban Church Planting. Look over the schedule. It is important that you understand the overall schedule for the times we are together. If you have any questions on the overall schedule, please direct them to: [Name and contact information].

2. As Deans of [name of your Evangel School], we would like you to read over the two outlines on coaching from the Evangel Dean Handbook (attached). Please read over the outline entitled "The Coach and the Church Plant Team at Evangel." The outline is only ten pages, pay attention especially to page 153 ("Team Evaluation Form"). You will receive copies of this page for each of the teams you assess at Evangel and it will be used to help you determine if the team is ready to be chartered.

3. Attached are also two documents about charters. The first is the one-page charter you will help each team work on during

Evangel. This is the one-page summary of their vision, values, and first-year strategy. Please review the document entitled "Evangel Church Plant Charter-2015." This is the single most important page (out of the many pages you will see when you get to boot camp). If you only read one page, read this page. Also review the three-page explanation of charters from the Evangel Dean Training entitled "Seminar: Charters, Coaches, and the Ongoing PWR Process" (attached).

Grace,

[Signature]

Sample Letter for Coaches Meetings at Evangel

Greetings Evangel Assessor and Field Coach,

Praise the Lord for your willingness to serve as an Evangel Coach! We settled on a schedule for special meetings, and I wanted all of you to be aware of them.

Special Coaches Meetings:

1. Coaches Orientation. Thursday night at Dinner (If you miss this meeting, please check in with [name of Dean] when you arrive at [name of Evangel School]).

2. First night at Evangel School: Each Coach will have opportunity to present how their team is doing and discuss any questions or concerns they have about the team they are responsible for evaluating ("staff" their team).

3. Second day: Coaches meeting to discuss any red flags about your team; opportunity to staff particular problems or opportunities you see with team.

4. Final Coaches meeting to confirm team's readiness to enter into the urban harvest field; sign certificates.

5. Celebration/Commissioning Service: note you will be taking pictures with your team.

Grace,

[Signature]

Sample Coaching Covenant

As your coach I promise to do the following:

- Enter into each coaching session prayerfully with an openness to the Holy Spirit.

- Work to gain your full trust by listening intently, asking clarifying questions, and keeping strict confidentiality (unless legally bound to share information due to its nature).

- Help you explore God's call for you...for today and for the future.

- Offer observations that may be helpful to you, always in a loving way.

- Offer knowledge and information that might be helpful.

- Never offer "answers" unless they have been specifically requested, and even then, they will be shared only after your own answers have been fully explored.

- Commit to meeting with you (either in person or by phone) one hour per month, and as special needs arise.

- I will monitor your commitment level as measured by tasks completed on time.

As a person being coached, I promise to do the following:

- Enter into each meeting prayerfully with an openness to the Holy Spirit.

- Openly share my thoughts and insights about my nature, my practices, and my passions (exploring who I am).

- Be open to your questions and your insights.

- Commit to meeting with you (either in person or by phone) one hour per month for one year.

- Carefully choose my commitments – then follow through on each of them.

Signed _____ Date _____